W9-BON-084

A Thousand Paths to Wisdom

A Thousand Paths to
wisdom

David Baird

MQP

Contents

Introduction

From the cradle to the grave, wisdom—or our lack of it—influences our daily lives, sometimes for the better, sometimes for the worse. It's easy to feel lost when setting out on the path to wisdom, but don't feel alone—since time began people, in the same situation, have left us their experiences, thoughts and advice. Collected in these pages are no fewer than

1000 thought-provoking, sometimes amusing, sometimes cryptic, and always wise thoughts distilled from many voices and minds over the centuries. Hopefully these offerings will start you on the path to wisdom. One thing is certain, we will all come out of it a little bit wiser.

Wise
Words

To know men is to be wise, to know oneself is to be illuminated.
To conquer men is to have strength, to conquer oneself is to be stronger still.
And to know when you have enough is to be rich.

It is better to suffer wrong than to do it, and happier to be sometimes cheated than not to trust.

Everything that happens was once a dream.

Those who come to wisdom through failure tend to be good people for that very reason.

Wisdom is about learning to keep those people who hate you as far away as possible from those who are as yet undecided.

Mind moves matter.

The problems of today will only be solved when we resolve ourselves to focus on tomorrow.

There can be no true success in a world of mediocrity.

A leader who does not hesitate before he sends his nation into battle is not fit to be a leader.

Only by his actions can a man make himself and his life whole.

Each individual is responsible for what they have done and for the people they have influenced.

A man's own natural duty, even if it seems imperfectly done, is better than work not naturally his own, even if it is well-performed.

It is not wise to be reckless with others, or to stand alone, stubborn against the multitude.

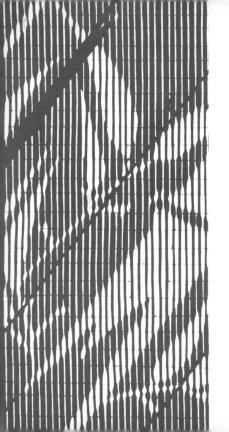

Have the courage to be wise— the path of wisdom is not an easy one to follow.

Genius is about developing the ability to perceive in an unhabitual way.

It is possible to act in a way that will give your friends no occasion for regret and your foes no cause for joy.

The heart seems to have its reasons which even reason cannot understand.

We can become wise only when we have learned to regard all men as equal. There can be no wisdom in prejudice.

The most crucial step toward solving a problem is to be able to recognize yourself as part of the problem.

The first duty of men is to take none of the principles of conduct upon trust and to do nothing without a clear and individual conviction that it is right to be done.

We must use time creatively, in the knowledge that the time is always ripe to do right.

The candle of love may burn out quickly but the flame of wisdom will burn forever.

There are those who seek to destroy and discredit you. Let them try, they can only make you stronger.

Knowledge is the ultimate antidote to fear.

Wisdom can only be acquired by the sustained development of an inquiring mind.

Forgiveness is a permanent state of being, not just an occasional act.

From hearing comes wisdom, from speaking, repentance.

No man is born wise, wisdom cannot be learned, it is a journey of discovery where the destination remains unknown.

Nothing in life can be profitable to you that makes you break a promise.

Morality is the observance of the rights of others.

Early to bed and early to rise makes a man healthy, wealthy, and wise.

Wisdom goes not always by years.

Like the bee gathering honey from different flowers, the wise man accepts the essence of different Scriptures and sees only the good in all religions.

Wisdom is neither inheritance nor legacy.

The wise man is more to be envied than a rich man.

Without wisdom, wealth is worthless.

Want of wisdom is more to be pitied than want of possessions.

A wise man never needs a weapon.
The mind is mightier than the fist.

The wise man is never less alone than
when he is by himself.

Well goes the case when wisdom
counsels.

Wisdom is the most invincible kind of strength, it lends the highest authority to action.

Don't concentrate on the folly of others—he is not wise who is not wise for himself.

Wisdom teaches the value of things and the wise person cares not for what they cannot have.

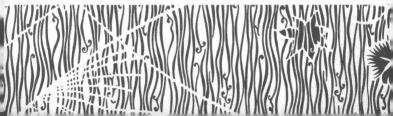

It is a great point of wisdom to find out one's own folly.

Learning is not wisdom—
you can learn to pick a lock
or steal a neighbor's car
but it would be wiser to
do neither.

Riches serve a wise man but command a fool.

The fool wanders, the wise man travels.

The wise seek wisdom, a fool has found it.

He that is a wise man by day is no fool by night.

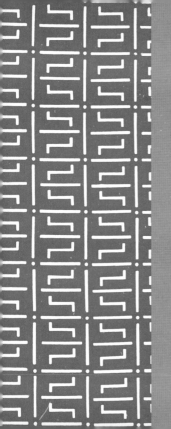

What the fool
does in the end,
the wise person
does at the
beginning.

Wisdom is
not wisdom
that has not
come through
mistakes.

A wise man may change his mind
frequently while the fool stands fast,
determined not to do so.

A wise man needs not blush for
changing his purpose.

No man can play the fool so well as the
wise man.

The wise propose, but fools determine.

Reason governs the wise man and cudgels the fool.

The first degree of folly is to hold oneself wise, the second to profess it, the third to despise counsel.

Trouble brings experience and experience brings wisdom.

Wisdom will only increase with attempts made to destroy it.

No one can be wise at all times, and even the wisest man may fall.

There can be no true success in a world of mediocrity.

Next time you consider fleeing from a problem, consider the acorn. It stood firm and it became an oak tree.

Before you can hope to be wise you must start at the very beginning, and learn to see things as they truly are.

**Problems
need
solutions.
Solutions
breed
new
problems.**

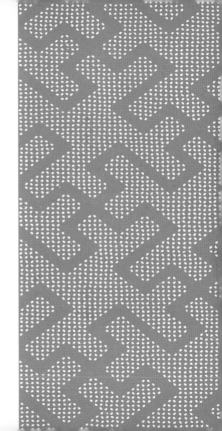

Salvation is a process that begins on earth and ends in eternity.

The process of salvation must come from within.

Salvation is not putting a man into heaven, but putting heaven into a man.

The cure for false theology is common sense.

We are reborn into this world every time we wake; there is daily the chance to make a new start and live a new life.

A thing cannot be and not be. Do not be fooled by illusion and false promises.

Wisdom is about looking outward as much as looking inward, and looking forward as much as looking backward.

With every opportunity that is missed, another one is born.

Most duels have their winner
but the one that will go on
forever is the duel between
yes and no.

You can melt ice to make cold water,
you can heat the cold water to make
hot water, but it cannot be all three
at once.

Freedom travels slowly—
from precedent to precedent.

Wisdom lies in knowing
when, and when not, to act.

Wisdom is knowing
which questions to ask.

The wise person knows
that no answer is also
an answer.

Complete wisdom is as rare as
complete folly.

The wise man will always make more opportunities than he finds.

Don't be so determined in your pursuit of wisdom that you forget to live a little along the way.

The wise man does not laugh to avoid weeping.

There are those who build houses to live in and those who build houses for others to look at.

Wisdom is like the darkness. In darkness all colors can agree.

When you live your life in a world of illusion it is good to know which door to go through to get back to reality.

The wise avoid short-term measures. Short-term measures taken today become the long-term problems of the future.

Beware.
Nothing is
more revealing
about a
person's
character
than their
pastimes and
amusements.

Understand that although we may well wish to do what we are supposed to do, circumstances will conspire to ensure that it is not always possible.

Wisdom is best seen in hindsight.

The wise person knows that there is sometimes more power in words left unsaid.

Words are potent weapons
for all causes, good or bad.

Procrastination
is the thief of time.

It is perhaps our delusions of adequacy which lead us to let not only ourselves but others down.

To speak, and to speak well, are two things. A fool may talk, but a wise man speaks.

Admire genius but beware—when genius is around everything is at risk.

Genius is not the same thing as wisdom. Genius is a gift, wisdom is a craft.

A true friend is one who knows all about you and who chooses to love you just the same.

If you can understand just one thing thoroughly, then you will understand everything.

Wise words don't come cheap.

A man who can see will move forward more surely than a blind man with a trustworthy guide, just as a person following an enlightened understanding will tread more surely than one following an obedience to custom.

He that is truly wise and great, lives both too early and too late.

Better an empty room than a bad lodger.

The only thing that the truly wise person
can be sure of is that they know nothing.

The wise person
is always willing to
see with the eyes
of a child.

Wisdom suffocates in a closed mind.

One cannot make all the clever people good—neither is it possible to make all the good people clever.

There is no bigger fool than the person that boasts of their wisdom.

There is great wisdom in being able to realize that you don't understand something before it goes too far.

The wise man is like a tree whose roots are fed from the earth while its branches rise toward heaven.

It is far better to be than to know.

They
that are
truly
wise
never
finish
learning.

Why should it be so difficult for us to admit we are wrong when there is nothing more helpful to resolving a problem than doing so?

Choosing the path of wisdom is not the easy option.

Follow reason as far as it will go, the path gets stonier as wisdom increases.

Pearls of
Wisdom

Give your all to the thing that is in front of you and once done, do the same with the thing behind it, and the next, and the next.

If you start something—finish it.

Thought comes free to those with no money.

You only get out of life what you are prepared to put into it.

It is far better to keep your mouth shut and be considered a fool by others rather than open it and remove all their doubts!

You can't keep a good man down.

Always admit it when you're wrong.

If you want to win the race—run faster than anybody else.

Try not to make a major decision when you are tired—or drunk.

**The bigger they come
the harder they fall.**

There are those that sit and talk about
what they dream of doing and others
who go out and do something about it.

**You may think that you can't
have your cake and eat it—
but sometimes you can.**

The more I want to
get something done,
the less I call it work.

Try not to make heavy weather
of things.

**If you overestimate or underestimate
the value of personal relationships
you may be in for a shock.**

Before you act, think about what effect
your actions will have.

Be careful if you don't know where you're going—you may never get there.

Misfortune never misses.

The same earth can become a hole and a hill at the same time.

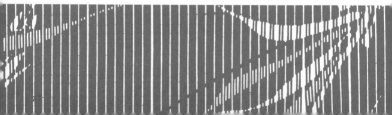

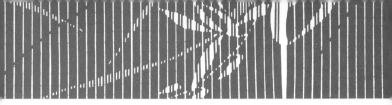

Conclusions usually happen
when we're tired of thinking.

**A celebrity is a person who is
known merely for being well known.**

It takes great wisdom to admit
that something is impossible.

When I don't know
what I'm doing—I
am doing research.

If you want to
be a winner
you must keep
on competing.

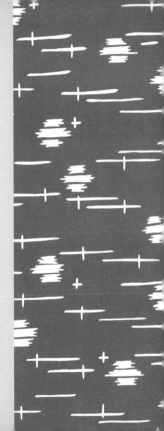

Don't hang your targets after
you've done your shooting.

Your feet might get muddy
but you won't get your hands
dirty reaching for the stars.

Experts, it seems, know more
about less and absolutely
everything about nothing.

Everybody has their day, it's just that some days seem to last longer than others.

You can win by telling lies or be defeated on principle.

Freedom is a chance to be even better.

If you don't like pressure stay away from jewelers.

You can't know you've reached the boundaries of what is possible without going beyond into the realm of the impossible.

The world, it seems, has become addicted to self-improvement—but is it any better for it?

Embrace change—don't run from it.

Every man is an architect, each designing their future, always running late and over budget and rarely getting the chance to enjoy the result.

95% of our time seems to be focused upon the problems and only 5% on finding solutions.

Reality has a way of cramping some people's style.

Consider the man who dug so long for treasure, that he missed the treasure of life and his hole became his grave.

Are you hesitating or simply
nailed to the floor?

**Einstein said "The secret to
creativity is knowing how
to hide your sources."**

Most of life is choice—the rest is pure luck.

Don't spend so long concentrating on putting one foot in front of the other that you forget to look where you are going.

Words can be extremely useful when ideas fail.

There will always be people who are against you whether you are right or wrong.

Success does not always equal skill.

More important than seeing the future is knowing the present.

Things always seem to take longer than you expect, even when you allow additional time in just such an expectation.

Man's desires are insatiable.

There's no such thing as a free ride.

You can take any road you like, but if you don't know where you're going, that's where you'll end up.

Man does before he speaks before he thinks.

Learn to
expect to
get what
you
deserve
rather
than what
you want.

With love and patience, nothing is impossible.

When will we learn that the world rules us—we can't rule the world.

You can't predict your future but you can invent it.

Wisdom is being able to foretell a mistake and avoid it. Experience is recognizing the same mistake every time you make it.

The wise general looks at all the battles that matter and commits to the one he can win.

Don't let fear stop you.

The average person thinks he isn't average at all.

The boxer is not afraid of being knocked down—he's afraid of not being able to get up again.

Be nice to the people you meet on your way up, you're bound to bump into them again on your way down.

We live in an insecure world filled with opportunity.

Better an authentic loser than a false success.

It's a poor show when the leader is struggling to catch up with the others.

It took a particular kind of wisdom to look out across all that sea and know there would be land to discover.

We are all actors in our own lives—
and there are no understudies.

**Wisdom is gleaned from those who,
through history, have chosen to
write about what mankind has done
and not about what he ought to
have done.**

The wise accept that fortunes come
tumbling into some men's laps.

Hope might be a good breakfast, but it makes a very poor supper.

Riches should serve a purpose, rather than the purpose serve them.

Death is the least of all evils.

It is not the lie that passes from your mind, but the one that sinks in and takes root that does the greatest harm.

The sooner we can accept that the things that we think and feel are mostly quite normal and commonplace, the sooner we can be truthful about ourselves.

In the kingdom of the blind the one-eyed man is king.

Wisdom is a treasure for all time.

What hope
is there
when
people,
even in front
of the
evidence,
turn their
head?

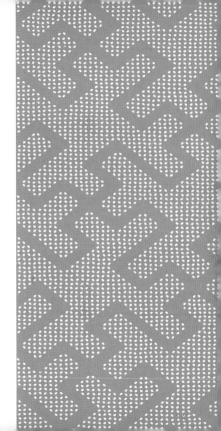

Never forsake old friends
for new.

**Old age is like a plane
flying through a storm.
Once you're aboard there's
nothing you can do.**

Don't think—do.

Freedom means nothing
if its meaning is
misunderstood.

Make reason your guide.

It is often the small actions of our daily lives that, over time, have the greatest influence on the world.

Act in the living present.

To stand still on the summit of perfection is difficult, and in the natural course of things, what cannot go forward slips back.

Wisdom is the supreme
part of happiness.

Genius is about the
conquering of chaos
and mystery.

Wisdom is about being able to break an enemy's resistance without the need for fighting.

To live in fear of death is many times to die.

Wisdom lies in thoughts not things.

You can be shown the path to wisdom, but only you can make the first step.

There is nothing nobler than humanity.

Nothing great has ever been achieved without enthusiasm.

Those who spend their time worrying about what people think of them wouldn't worry if they knew how rarely other people think of them.

One thought can change the world.

The wiser you become the less you admit to knowing.

The wise man knows it's all just a game.

Only one person can tell you what wisdom means, and that is you.

Remember. You are the master of your own fate, the captain of your own soul.

Motion is motion and action is action. Never mistake one for the other.

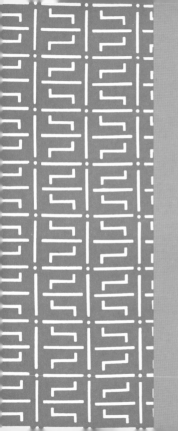

Wisdom lies in
understanding
not only the big
things, but also
the little things
in life.

Freedom of the mind is the greatest form of freedom that exists.

Wisdom is its own reward.

Wisdom is knowing that silence often speaks louder than words.

The question to ask yourself is this: If life would let you attempt to do something that you knew would not fail, what would it be?

One enemy is too many— one hundred friends are too few.

There is no strength in absence.

In order to become better than anybody else you must first become better than yourself.

Wisdom is one word that means something different to everyone.

Life is like a game of cards. It's not so much about what you're holding but how you play what you've been dealt.

Never allow what you cannot do
interfere with what you can do.

**If you pray for rain, be prepared
to be struck by lightning.**

Life involves passions, faiths, doubts,
and courage—in unequal measures.

**The easiest person to deceive
is yourself.**

No matter how
simple the task,
there is always
someone who will
find the wrong way
to do it.

Whether it's bad, or good, it won't last long.

Do, or do not. There is no try.

It is often better to delay than get it wrong.

Compromise does not mean cowardice.

Life is filled with insurmountable opportunities.

It's extremely difficult to fake wisdom—even if you're very good at pretending to be serious.

Monuments are made
to those who don't
need them.

It's not what they
take away from
you but what
you do with the
rest.

The most frightening thing about any given situation is being able to do nothing about it.

A man who has made a mistake and doesn't correct it, is making another mistake.

It's not over
until it's over.

Advice

Twenty years from now you will be more disappointed by the things you didn't do than by the things you did do.

The best medicine in life is a faithful friend.

Opportunities multiply as they are seized.

Enemies come to those who make changes.

If you set off in search of the pot of gold at the end of the rainbow make sure that you know which end it's at.

Never go to bed thinking about what to complain about tomorrow.

Good advice is rather like medicine—it might leave an unpleasant taste in the mouth but it can do a lot of good.

It may be possible to deceive those better than you but never your peers.

You will never be disappointed if you go through life always expecting the worst, but you'll miss out on a lot of fun along the way.

It's no good wandering through life wanting to be someone, you have to be clear who that someone is that you want to be.

Silence is the cornerstone of character.

Put yourself out on a limb now and then, that way you'll stand a chance of reaching the fruit.

Do what you've always done and you will always be what you have always been.

Try once—this will help you to get over the fear of doing something.

Try twice—this will enable you to learn to do it.

Try three times—this way you will be able to see if you like doing it or not.

Begin at once to live, and count each separate day as a separate life.

Readiness is all.

When the time comes to tell your children how it is they came to be born it would be wise to know the reason.

Love thy neighbor as thyself.

Count your blessings and not another's.

Try and do one thing each day that you would really rather not do.

You can't do better than your best.

It is better to lead by example than by decree.

Hold on to your friends for friendship is the most important thing in times of adversity as well as in times of happiness.

Read much, but draw your own conclusions.

It doesn't matter what you do in life so long as you do it as well as possible.

To your own self be true.

Enjoy your work or find work you can enjoy.

You've got a brain, so use it.

Always listen to children.

Never contend with a man who has nothing to lose.

Live to study don't study to live.

Never do yourself the thing that you criticize in others.

Don't walk on thin ice.

When your past life chills you, burn a few bridges and warm yourself in the flames.

When you don't have a solution you can always admire the problem.

It is better to be alone than to be found in bad company.

Don't wait until the roses wither before you place them in your hair.

He who has begun his task is half way done. Have the courage to begin!

Dare to live—don't just spend your life avoiding death.

Don't do anything which will cause you fear if it becomes known to your neighbor.

When in doubt if an action is good or bad, refrain.

It is unwise to take more in life than you can use.

Choose how to act when there is a clear choice between good and bad consequences.

Live well, laugh often, and love much.

Try to make your prologues shorter than your stories.

Don't just criticize, go and help.

Don't waste your energy in being indignant.

If you don't accept defeat you cannot be defeated.

In all respects, and with all people, treat others as you yourself wish to be treated.

Always own up. Errors multiply when concealed.

It's fine to believe in miracles but fatal to come to rely upon them.

If it's worth doing then it's worth doing well.

When everybody is busy beating their own drum, the important thing is to march to the beat of yours and not someone else's.

Take care when taking advice from others.

If you pretend to have knowledge that you don't possess you'd better avoid the experts.

Do your best with what's on offer.

If you have nothing pleasant to say about someone, it is best to say nothing at all.

Lose your temper and you lose the battle.

Don't yearn for the impossible.

When you believe in a cause,
never give up.

Be yourself—nobody can be you
better than you.

Live each day that dawns as if it is your last.

It is wise to follow the truth wherever it leads.

The lashes of the tongue are far more severe than any whip.

Dare to be wise; begin to live.

Do as you would be done by.

Save your money or spend it wisely.

If you are certain you are right, go straight ahead.

Let nobody deter you from doing what you believe is right.

You're every bit as good as the next person—all you've got to do is prove it!

Try to see yourself as others see you, and be prepared for a nasty surprise.

Always keep a few miles between you and your relations.

Never resist a challenge.

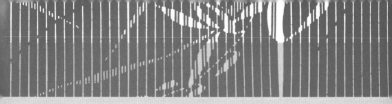

If there's something that you have always wanted to do but have been putting it off until the right time—do it, and do it now!

Never make a promise unless you mean to stick by it.

You should never want something so badly that it hurts if you don't ever get it.

Do right and you need fear no man.

It is not possible to get anxious about the past so there is little point in becoming depressed about the future.

Don't put off until tomorrow what you can do today.

Look at all things as they are.

It is as well to create good precedents as to follow them.

In all human nature there exists less of the wise and more of the fool.

You can defy everything but age. You will only look foolish if you try.

We all fail at many things, many times in this life but we don't become failures, until we start blaming someone else.

Never allow what you cannot do to interfere with what you can do.

Read, weigh, and consider.

In order to become better than anybody else you must first become better than yourself.

It's what you do with what you know that gets you paid!

Fill your garden with fruits and it will always be filled with birdsong.

Ensure that during your lifetime you do something for posterity.

Choice is not always an easy option to choose.

Give yourself more alternatives and that way you will have more choice.

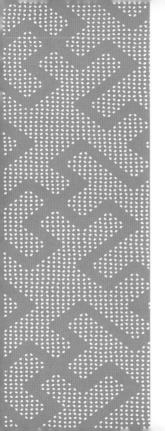

The most
important thing
to know is your
own mind.

Just as there are
unhappy lies, so too
there is happy
invention.

Time does not stand still for anyone. As the times change, so too can you.

One should not always try to take giant leaps in life when the rest of mankind will be perfectly satisfied with every small step you take.

The wise never rush into despair—it is easier to find your way in than out.

Always have something positive to say.

Allow yourself only to forget
through choice.

If you fall seven times, stand
up eight.

Live your life as though you intend to live forever.

Conduct your affairs as though you expect to die tomorrow.

It is said that fools rush in. Sometimes it is best to wait and see.

If you travel the path of your choice, be prepared to lend your critics a pen.

If you want to set an example, try patience—for it is often perceived as genius.

When you can't seem to reach an agreement it is often wiser to agree to disagree.

Liberty is one of the greatest treasures to mankind. Never give up your liberties lightly.

Your solitude should be voluntary.

Remember that the impossible takes a little bit longer.

When your entire world seems upside down you can either attempt to put it right again or stand on your head.

Anybody with the capacity to please has the potential to annoy.

When you make a mistake, take another chance—only when you chose not to do so do you fail.

A single moment of wrath can turn the universe to ashes.

Even the wise never know when coincidence might strike.

It is a great gift to know when to remain silent.

Better a good loser than a bad winner.

If you have to be something then be as it is you wish to seem.

Only the honorable can associate with the honorable.

Find friendship with yourself—until you can it will be difficult to find friendship with anyone else.

When people say they hate you for what you are, tell them that it feels better than being loved for what you are not.

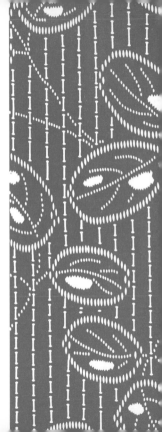

Famous
Voices

If there were no falsehood in the world,
there would be no doubt,
If there were no doubt there would be
no inquiry;
If no inquiry, no wisdom, no knowledge,
no genius.

Walter Savage Landor

**To know how to grow old is the
master work of wisdom,
and one of the most difficult
chapters in the great art of living.**

Henri Frédéric Amiel

To ask the hard
question is simple.
W. H. Auden

Our deeds determine us as much as we determine our deeds.

George Eliot

The deed is everything, the glory is naught.

Johann Wolfgang von Goethe

The more we do the
more we can do; the
more busy we are the
more leisure we have.

William Hazlitt

**The actions of
men are the best
interpreters of
their thoughts.**

John Locke

I prefer the errors of enthusiasm to the indifference of wisdom.

Anatole France

Folly is wisdom spun too fine.

Benjamin Franklin

Good people are good because they've come to wisdom through failure.

William Saroyan

Doubt is the vestibule through which all must pass before they can enter into the temple of wisdom.

Charles Caleb Colton

There are moments when everything goes well, but don't be frightened, it won't last.

Jules Renard

It may serve as a comfort to us, in all our calamities and afflictions, that he that loses anything and gets wisdom by it is a gainer by the loss.

Sir Roger L'Estrange

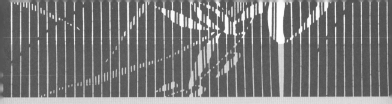

Deliberate with caution but act with decision and yield with graciousness or oppose with firmness.

Charles Caleb Colton

To learn moderation is the essence of sound sense and real wisdom.

Jacques Bénigne Bossuet

Knowledge is proud
that he has learned
so much; wisdom is
humble that he knows
no more.

William Cowper

Be humble, if thou would'st attain to wisdom. Be humbler still, when Wisdom thou hast mastered.

Helena Petronova Blavatsky

The bird of wisdom flies low, and seeks her food under hedges; the eagle himself would be starved if he always soared aloft and against the sun.

Walter Savage Landor

Every man feels instinctively that all the beautiful sentiments in the world weigh less than a single lovely action.

James Lowell

It is the mark of a good action that it appears inevitable in retrospect.
Robert Louis Stevenson

Good actions ennoble us, we are the sons of our own deeds.

Miguel de Cervantes

Words may show a man's wit but actions his meaning.

Benjamin Franklin

He who considers too much will perform little.

Friedrich Schiller

A loving heart is the truest wisdom.
Charles Dickens

The first sign of love is the last of wisdom.
Antoine Bret

Solitude is the best nurse of wisdom.
Laurence Sterne

Caution is the eldest child of wisdom.
Victor Hugo

Honesty is the
first chapter of
the book of
wisdom.
Thomas Jefferson

But what is liberty without wisdom, and without virtue? It is the greatest of all possible evils; for it is folly, vice and madness, without tuition or restraint.

Edmund Burke

Knowledge is convertible into power, and axioms into rules of utility and duty. But knowledge itself is not power. Wisdom is power; and her prime minister is justice, which is the perfected law of truth.

Albert Pike

What is strength without a double
share of wisdom? Vast, unwieldy,
burdensome, proudly secure, yet liable
to fall by weakest subtleties; strength's
not made to rule, but to subserve,
where wisdom bears command.

John Milton

We can be knowledgeable with
other men's knowledge but
we cannot be wise with other
men's wisdom.

Michel de Montaigne

Knowledge comes,
but wisdom lingers.

Alfred Lord Tennyson

Studies teach not their own use; that is a wisdom without and above them, won by observation.

Francis Bacon

Knowledge dwells in heads replete with thoughts of other men; wisdom in minds attentive to their own.

William Cowper

He's a fool that cannot conceal
his wisdom.

Benjamin Franklin

The motto of chivalry is also
the motto of wisdom; to serve
all, but love only one.

Honoré de Balzac

The law is the last result of human wisdom acting upon human experience for the benefit of the public.

Samuel Johnson

Justice without wisdom is impossible.

James Anthony Froude

The divine essence itself is love
and wisdom.

Emanuel Swedenborg

**Wisdom is ofttimes nearer when we
stoop than when we soar.**

William Wordsworth

Moderation is the inseparable
companion of wisdom but with it
genius has not even a nodding
acquaintance.

Charles Caleb Colton

By wisdom
wealth is
won;
But riches
purchased
wisdom yet
for none.
Bayard Taylor

The power is yours, but not the sight;
You see not upon what you tread;
You have the ages for your guide,
But not the wisdom to be led.

Edwin A. Robinson

Wisdom is only found in truth.

Johann Wolfgang von Goethe

Man is never helped in his suffering by what he thinks for himself but only by revelation of a wisdom greater than his own. It is this which lifts him out of his distress.

Carl Gustav Jung

Wisdom and goodness are twin-born, one heart must hold both sisters, never seen apart.

William Cowper

The most evident token and apparent sign of true wisdom is a constant and unconstrained rejoicing.

Michel de Montaigne

The strongest symptom of wisdom in man is his being sensible of his own follies.

François La Rochefoucauld

A prudent question is one-half of wisdom.

Francis Bacon

The doorstep to the temple of wisdom is a knowledge of our own ignorance.

Charles Spurgeon

Common sense in an uncommon degree
is what the world calls wisdom.

Samuel Taylor Coleridge

**Nine tenths of wisdom consists in
being wise in time.**

Theodore Roosevelt

To admit ignorance is to exhibit wisdom.

Ashley Montagu

Books give not wisdom where none was before,
but where some is, their reading makes it more.

John Harrington

The wisdom of
the wise and
the experience
of ages may
be preserved
by quotation.
Benjamin Disraeli

The world is all gates, all opportunities, strings of tension waiting to be struck.

Ralph Waldo Emerson

Hatred is self-punishment.

Hosea Ballou

To be angry is to revenge the faults of others on ourselves.

Alexander Pope

Anger is a wind which blows out the lamp of the mind.

Robert G. Ingersoll

An ill-humored man is a prisoner at the mercy of an enemy from whom he can never escape.

SA'DI

Cunning to wisdom is as an ape to man.

William Penn

The man who does not read good books has no advantage over the man who cannot read them.

Mark Twain

There are more fools than wise men; and even in wise men, more folly than wisdom.

Sébatien-Roch Nicolas Chamfort

A man with one watch knows what time it is. A man with two watches is never sure.

John Peer

Only two things are infinite, the universe and human stupidity, and I'm not sure about the former.

Albert Einstein

Nothing is more intolerable than to have to admit to yourself your own errors.

Ludwig van Beethoven

Only those who dare to fail greatly can ever achieve greatly.

Robert F. Kennedy

If you're strong enough, there are no precedents.

F. Scott Fitzgerald

If at first you don't succeed, try, and try again. Then give up. There's no sense in being a damned fool about it.

W. C. Fields

The reward of a thing well done is to have done it.

Ralph Waldo Emerson

I find that the harder I work, the more luck I seem to have.

Thomas Jefferson

Truth comes out of error more easily than out of confusion.

Francis Bacon

You can run with the big dogs or sit on the porch and bark.

Wallace Arnold

Computers are
useless. They
can only give
you answers.
Pablo Picasso

**The sum of wisdom is that time is
never lost that is devoted to work.**
Ralph Waldo Emerson

It is easy for men to write and talk like philosophers, but to act with wisdom, there is the rub!

Antoine de Rivaroli

To be a philosopher is not merely to have subtle thoughts; but so to love wisdom as to live according to its dictates.

Henry David Thoreau

Do not wait for extraordinary circumstances to do good action; try to use ordinary situations.

Johann Paul Friedrich Richter

To act with common sense, according to the moment, is the best wisdom; and the best philosophy is to do one's duties, to take the world as it comes, submit respectfully to one's lot, bless the goodness that has given us so much happiness with it, whatever it is.

Horace Walpole

The great end of life is not
knowledge but action.

Thomas Huxley

Opportunity is missed by most
people because it is dressed in
overalls and looks like work.

Thomas Alva Edison

No problem can withstand the assault of sustained thinking.

Voltaire

Well done is better than well said.

Benjamin Franklin

Wisdom is to the mind what health is to the body.

François La Rochefoucauld

The weak have remedies, the wise have joys; superior wisdom is superior bliss.

Edward Young

Nothing in life is to be feared. It is only to be understood.

Marie Curie

Great spirits have always encountered violent opposition from mediocre minds.

Albert Einstein

Kites rise highest against the wind—not with it.

Winston Churchill

If a man will begin with certainties, he shall end in doubts; but if he will be content to begin with doubts, he shall end in certainties.

Francis Bacon

A man's wisdom is his best friend; folly, his worst enemy.

William Temple

Man usually avoids attributing cleverness to somebody else—unless it is an enemy.

Albert Einstein

There is one thing stronger than all the armies in the world, and that is an idea whose time has come.

Victor Hugo

Wisdom alone is true ambition's aim.
Wisdom the source of virtue, and of fame,
Obtained with labor, for mankind employed,
And, then, when most you share it, best enjoyed.

Alfred North Whitehead

Thinking is easy but acting is difficult and to put one's thoughts into action is the most difficult thing in the world.

Johann Wolfgang von Goethe

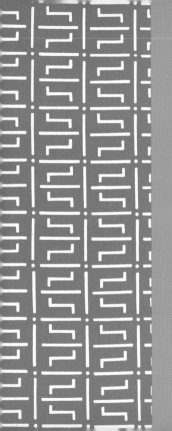

There are but two
things worth living
for: to do what is
worthy of being
written; and to
write what is
worthy of being
read; and greater of
these is the doing.

Albert Pike

Our only true course is to let the motive
for action be in the action itself, never in
its reward; not to be incited by the
hope of the result, nor yet indulge a
propensity for inertness.

Helena Petronova Blavatsky

Each morning sees some task begun,
Each evening sees it close;
Something attempted, something done,
Has earned a night's repose.

Henry Wadsworth Longfellow

Idleness is the
holiday of fools.
G. K. Chesterton

Beauty is the index of a larger fact
in wisdom.

Oliver Wendell Holmes

The reasonable man adapts himself to the world; the unreasonable one persists in trying to adapt the world to himself. Therefore, all progress depends on the unreasonable man.

George Bernard Shaw

They whom truth and wisdom lead
Can gather honey from a weed.

William Cowper

Our acts make or mar us, we
are the children of our deeds.

Victor Hugo

Man's main task in life is to give
birth to himself.

Erich Fromm

Be happy. It is a way of being wise.

Colette

Human felicity is produced not so much by great pieces of good fortune that seldom happen, as by little advantages that occur every day.

Benjamin Franklin

Life is a great bundle of little things.

Oliver Wendell Holmes

Life is what happens to you when you're busy making other plans.

John Lennon

When one is trying to do something beyond one's known powers it is useless to seek the approval of friends. Friends are at their best in moments of defeat.

Henry Miller

You should treat all disasters as if they were trivialities but never treat a triviality as if it were a disaster.

Quentin Crisp

Blessed is he who expects nothing, for he shall never be disappointed.

Alexander Pope

A stumble may prevent a fall.

Thomas Fuller

When a man has not a good reason for doing a thing, he has one good reason for letting it alone.

Walter Scott

The best way to avoid a bad action is by doing a good one, for there is no difficulty in the world like that of trying to do nothing.

John Clare

The art of being wise is the art
of knowing what to overlook.

William James

**It has been by experience that
people who have no vices have
very few virtues.**

Abraham Lincoln

The "silly question" is the first intimation of some totally new development.

Alfred North Whitehead

The greatest lesson in life is to know that even fools are right sometimes.

Winston Churchill

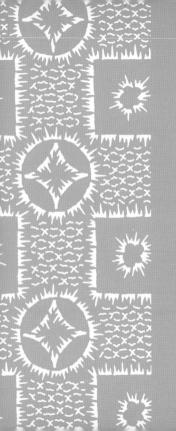

There is an element of truth in every idea that lasts long enough to be called corny.

Irving Berlin

A man should never be ashamed to own that he has been in the wrong, which is but saying, in other words, that he is wiser today than he was yesterday.

Johnathan Swift

When one God dwells in all living beings, then why do you hate others? Why do you frown at others? Why do you become indignant towards others? Why do you use harsh words? Why do you try to rule and domineer over others? Why do you exploit folly? Is this not sheer ignorance? Get wisdom and rest in peace.

Sivananda

Some
Thoughts

You can bet on a winning horse—
but you can never bet enough on a
winning horse.

If it's not worth doing then it's
not worth doing well.

Bravery and stupidity go hand
in hand.

A powerful imagination is something to strive for.

The only ones who can fool all of the people all of the time are working for the leading advertising agencies.

The boardroom is rather like the bedroom—only success in the boardroom can usually be achieved by faking sincerity.

Man does ten times the work he used to do because he's come to realize that nine times out of ten he's wrong.

Good health and a bad memory for some spells of happiness.

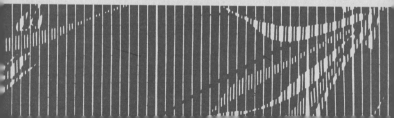

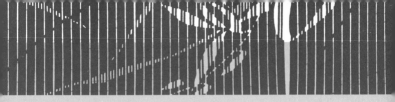

Ignorance and confidence have led many to success.

Whichever way you look at it, in order to succeed another must fail.

To motivate ourselves or indeed others, the quickest and most sure way is to take the imagination by storm.

It's no good wandering through life wanting to be someone, you have to be clear who that someone is.

There are those who go through life never making an error and there are those who go through life making many undetected errors.

There are two approaches to life: The carelessly planned life that leads to everything taking three times longer than anticipated; and the carefully planned life, where everything only takes twice as long.

Wisdom tells us that the same mistake is likely to occur again.

When a thing ceases to be a subject
of controversy, it ceases to be a subject
of interest.

Forgetting is equally as important as remembering.

No true autobiography has been or will
ever be written. We all have things that
we are afraid to tell about ourselves.

You exercise your right of choice every
time you choose not to decide.

People spend a fortune on trying to improve their looks when the best beauty treatment comes free in the form of a smile.

The longest road out is the shortest road home.

Envy shortens life.

Allowing yourself to be bored is a criminal waste of life.

A hero is a man who does what he can.

Love has the power to bring out the absolute best—and worst—in all of us.

Those who arrive at wisdom through failure tend to have a much deeper grasp of its value.

The busiest people do not always get the most done.

Solutions need problems just as problems need solutions.

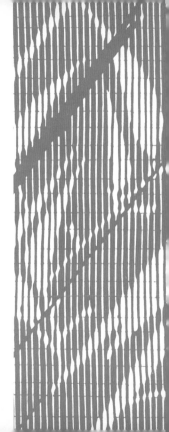

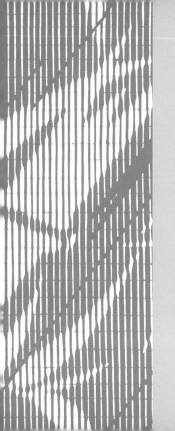

Politicians have a unique method of redefining success each time they don't succeed.

The gambler has a unique way of turning a thousand-to-one shot into a fifty-fifty chance.

It is still quite possible to enjoy doing those things that we're not very good at.

Boldness has genius, power, and magic in it.

Education is the key to freedom.

Pride is the most dangerous enemy anyone can have, it destroys us from the inside out.

They pay for your opinions and not your doubts.

Who are we if the thoughts we think are someone else's?

Greater understanding increases the capacity for tolerance.

Where there is a feast of words there is often a famine of wisdom.

It takes a hell of a lot of knowledge to really know how little you know.

The fool sees a thing, the wise watch.

They who have never loved, have never lived.

What is most contrary to salvation is not sin but habit.

Wisdom after the event is
no wisdom.

**We can criticize the weather but it
will take no notice.**

Lies are but the truth in masquerade.

That which is necessary is
never a risk.

A mistake is not the same as an error. We can make a mistake and correct it but it would be an error to knowingly make a mistake and do nothing about correcting it.

Desire is the stimulant of creativity.

Experience is the mother of wisdom.

A still tongue makes a wise head.

Little things please little minds.

Wisdom needs caution and confidence in equal balance.

You can of course quit while you're ahead—but quitters never win.

Everybody gets at least one opportunity in their life but it is often difficult to recognize it when it comes along.

While the ambitious strive to get ahead, the wise simply try to do the job they've been given well.

As a culture, we are too concerned with the spirit and have forgotten our soul.

Knowledge itself is power, power without wisdom is dangerous.

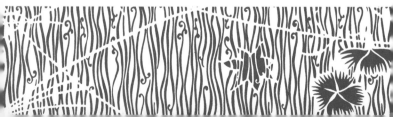

Those who don't know how to weep with their whole heart will never know how to laugh.

Some see life-long relationships and marriage as a destination while others view them as a means of traveling.

The most you can ever hope to do, is to do your best.

If you can imagine the thing you fear you are half way to confronting it, if you confront the thing you fear you are half way to conquering it.

The good opinion of fools is not worth the wear of winning.

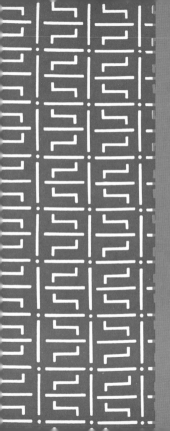

Follow your conscience.

Our intelligence is the thing that allows us to hold two opposing thoughts at the same time.

Is it always reasonable to be reasonable?

We are the sum of our experiences.

Without the rain there would be no meadows, without the shadow there would be no sunshine, without the bitter there would be no sweet.

Good temper is sometimes more irritating than bad temper.

All teachings that seek to bring our lives out from the darkness into the new light of being tend to leave great clouds of doubt.

Why is it that people insist on meeting a large and far reaching mind at its narrowest point?

The wise know that our judgement becomes impaired when our imagination goes blank.

**Is it really possible to be less than
God but more than man?**

Revenge is a form of wild justice which
merely doubles the original hurt.

Adversity has its hopes and comforts.

Vice is to prosperity what virtue is
to adversity.

**The world will always have the
need for people who can imagine
things that never were.**

It is perhaps unwise to only have your own company, for if you are always with yourself, you will inevitably become your own tormentor.

A closed mind is infinitely more difficult to open than a closed door.

Why is it that so many throughout history have been driven by the desire to seek power when it meant losing their liberty?

Severity breeds fear. Roughness breeds hate.

The bold are bad at keeping promises.

Wisdom brings natural authority.

With thought all our actions become intentional.

You can know light but can you imagine what will make light?

In charity there is no such thing as excess.

Avoiding superstition is in itself a superstitious act.

An open mind is the best traveling companion.

It is dangerous to accept a cunning man as wise.

It is not wise to argue with fools.

Some of the greatest thoughts in the history of mankind simply popped into people's heads unexpectedly.

The wise man does not set his house alight in his desire to eat toast.

If you wish to save time, choose time.

A crowd is the loneliest place to be.

Time is itself the greatest of innovators.

Suspicions are nocturnal creatures that inhabit the night-time of your thoughts.

Wealth is a burden, riches are for spending.

Some study for the pleasure of learning. Some study because it looks good on their resumé. Some study because it gives them ability.

He who knows little suspects much.

The mind is a garden that occasionally needs weeding.

The two most difficult moments of any project are the beginning and the end.

The only path that will lead us out of servitude to freedom is thought.

Any group or collective thought is only as strong as its weakest link.

Great acts are born of great thoughts.

It is impossible to learn and understand without thought.

We are where our thoughts have taken us, and we are going where they will take us tomorrow.

Arouse the mind, it is your most powerful tool.

It would be impossible to alter our life without first altering our thinking.

All our fears of life and fears of death can be dispelled through knowledge.

It takes great courage to avoid being touched by the centuries of evil doctrine that have accumulated around us.

With thought comes reason yet reason is a slave to passion.

Our thoughts are a paradise to which we can return at will.

Wisdom grows
from the same
seed as
common sense.

Every man's memory
is his private literature.

Aldous Huxley

You may be able to remember a great deal but are you wise enough to be able to forget?

Do not depend upon your memory alone, to do so will destroy your power of thought and it is thought that leads to wisdom.

Knowledge without wisdom is like a roof with no house beneath it.

Where there is learning untempered by experience, a weak judgement is to be discovered.

Imagination is creation.

Knowledge has a way of coming and going whereas wisdom tends to stick around.

Learn not to worry about things that you have no power to change. Worrying is destructive thought.

Imagination is the key that winds up the spring of the possible.

One is always free to imagine.

There is nothing quite so fulfilling as turning imagination into action.

One has to adapt one's thinking to the question at hand.

Imagination is a whole other universe where anything is possible.

Any situation worth understanding is confusing.

Ancient
Wisdom

Knowledge, the object of knowledge, and the knower are the three factors which motivate action; the senses, the work, and the doer comprise the threefold basis of action.

Bhagavad Gita

Heaven never helps the men who will not act.

Sophocles

Waste no more time arguing what a good man should be. Be one.

Marcus Aurelius

What one has, one ought to use: and whatever he does he should do with all his might.

Cicero

The unexamined life is not worth living.

Socrates

In seeking wisdom, the first stage
is silence, the second listening, the
third, remembrance, the fourth
practicing, the fifth, teaching.

Solomon Ibn Gabiro

Greed, lust, fear, anger, misfortune,
unhappiness all are derived from
foolishness. Thus foolishness is the
greatest of poisons.

Buddha

To do an evil act is base. To do a good one without incurring danger is common enough. But it is part of a good man to do great and noble deeds though he risks everything in doing them.

Plutarch

The superior man acts before he speaks, and afterwards speaks according to his action.

Confucius

To make no mistakes is not in the power of man; but from their errors and mistakes the wise and good learn wisdom for the future.

Plutarch

The good of the people is the chief law.

Cicero

The pine stays green in winter—
wisdom in hardship.

Chinese proverb

In youth and beauty wisdom is but rare!

Homer

Deceive boys with toys, but men with oaths.

Lysander

In wisdom and understanding we have
the archetypal positive and negative, the
primordial maleness and femaleness,
established while countenance "beheld
not" countenance and manifestation
was incipient. It is from these primary
pairs of opposites that the pillars of the
universe spring, between which is
woven the web of manifestation.

Kabbalah

There is nothing so absurd but some
philosopher has said it.

Cicero

Nature never says one thing, wisdom another.

Juvenal

For in every ill-turn of fortune the most unhappy sort of misfortune is to have been happy.

Boethius

Hatred is inveterate anger.

Cicero

Man is the measure of all things.

Protagoras

When you meet someone better than yourself, turn your thoughts to becoming his equal. When you meet someone not as good as you are, look within and examine your own self.

Confucius

As a plain garment best adorneth a beautiful woman, so decent behaviour is the best adornment of inner wisdom.

Akhenaton

Anger is momentary madness.

Horace

Famous men have the whole earth as their memorial.

Pericles

Not to be born is, past all prizing, best.

Sophocles

When a man dies, what does not leave him?
The voice of a dead man goes into fire, his
breath into wind, his eyes into the sun,
his mind into the moon, his hearing into the
quarters of heaven, his body into the earth,
his spirit into space, the hairs of his head
into plants, and his blood and semen are
placed in water, what then becomes of this
person? What remains is action. Its quality
becomes fate. Verily one becomes good by
good action, bad by bad action.

Upanishads

Of making many books there is no end; and much study is a weariness of the flesh.

Ecclesiastes 12:12

He gives the poor man twice as much good who gives quickly.

Publilius

The superior man seeks what is right; the inferior one, what is profitable.

Confucius

That deed is not well done of which a man must repent, and the reward of which he receives crying and with a tearful face. No, that deed is well done of which a man does not repent, and the reward of which he receives gladly and cheerfully.

The Dhammapada

For there is nothing sillier than a silly laugh.

Catullus

Better to do a good
deed near at home
than go far away to
burn incense.

Chinese proverb

**You can't step twice
into the same river.**

Heraclitus

Necessity gives the
law without itself
acknowledging one.

Publilius Syrus

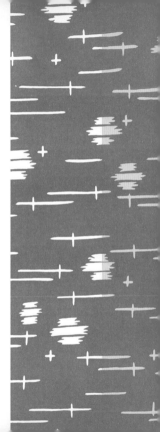

Live not as though there were a
thousand years ahead of you. Fate
is at your elbow; make yourself
good while life and power are
still yours.

Marcus Aurelius

Man is by nature a
political animal.

Aristotle

Men do not value a good deed
unless it brings a reward.

Ovid

**If you wish to reach the
highest, begin at the lowest.**

Publilius Syrus

It is a descending stream of
pure activity which is the
dynamic force of the universe.

Kabbalah

All human actions have one
or more of these seven
causes; chance, nature,
compulsions, habit, reason,
passion, desire.

Aristotle

Tragedy is thus a representation of an action that is worth serious attention, complete in itself and of some amplitude—by means of pity and fear bringing about the purgation of such emotions.

Aristotle

To talk goodness is not good—only to do it is.

Chinese proverb

I am a man, I count nothing human foreign to me.

Terence

To be doing good deeds is man's most glorious task.

Sophocles

A tree is known by its fruit; a man by his deeds. A good deed is never lost, he who sows courtesy reaps friendship and he who plants kindness gathers love.

Basil

How can he get wisdom whose talk is of bullocks?

Ecclesiasticus 38:25

You may drive out
nature with a
pitchfork, yet she'll be
constantly running
back.

Horace

Necessity is
the mother
of invention.
Plato

**Anyone can hold the helm
when the sea is calm.**

Publilius Syrus

They are able because they
think they are able.

Virgil

**There are as many opinions
as there are people: each
has his own correct way.**

Terence

A man is a wolf rather than a man to another man, when he hasn't yet found out what he's like.

Plautus

O fool fool! The pains which thou takest to hide what thou art are far more than would make thee what thou wouldst seem; and the children of wisdom shall mock at thy cunning when, in the midst of security thy disguise is stripped off, and the finger of derision shall point thee to scorn.

Akhenaton

The life so short, the craft so long to learn.

Hippocrates

Knowledge without justice ought to be called cunning rather than wisdom.

Plato

There are many wonderful things, and nothing is more wonderful than man.

Sophocles

Do not be frightened or bewildered by the luminous, brilliant, very sharp and clear light of supreme wisdom.

Tibetan Book of the Dead

Even as a caterpillar, when coming to an end of a blade of grass, reaches out to another blade of grass and draws itself over to it, in the same way the Soul, leaving the body and unwisdom behind, reaches out to another body and draws itself over to it.

Upanishads

It is fortune, not wisdom, that rules man's life.

Cicero

True wisdom is less presuming than folly. The wise man doubteth often, and changeth his mind; the fool is obstinate and doubteth not; he knoweth all things but his own ignorance.

Akhenaton

Poetry is something more philosophical and more worthy of serious attention than history.

Aristotle

**Great doubts
deep wisdom.
Small doubts
little wisdom.**

Chinese proverb

Where fear is present, wisdom
cannot be.

Lactantius

Into deep darkness fall those who
follow action.
Into deeper darkness fall those
who follow knowledge.
There are worlds of no joy, regions
of utter darkness.
To those worlds go after death
those who in their unwisdom
have not wakened up to light.

Upanishads

As the kindled fire consumes the fuel, so in the flame of wisdom the embers of action are burnt to ashes.

Bhagavad Gita

The man who makes everything that leads to happiness depend upon himself, and not upon other men, has adopted the very best plan for living happily. This is the man of moderation, the man of manly character and of wisdom.

Plato

Money has no smell.

Emperor Vespasian

Nothing can be created out of nothing.

Lucretius

**Silence at the proper season is
wisdom, and better than
any speech.**

Plutarch

On life's journey faith is nourishment, virtuous deeds a shelter, wisdom is the light by day and right mindfulness is the protection by night. If a man lives a pure life nothing can destroy him, if he has conquered greed nothing can limit his freedom.

Buddha

By suffering
comes wisdom.
Aeschylus

To be satisfied with a
little, is the greatest
wisdom; and he that
increaseth his riches,
increaseth his cares;
but a contented mind is
a hidden treasure, and
trouble findeth it not.
Akhenaton

Observation, not old age,
brings wisdom.

Publilius Syrus

As long as you watch the way,
As long as your steps are steady,
As long as your wisdom is unimpaired,
So long will you reap profit.

Nagarjuna

The king of truth is the king of kings. His ancestry is of the purest and the highest. He not only rules the four quarters of the world, but he is also lord of wisdom and protector of all virtuous teachings.

Buddha

Purity engenders wisdom, passion avarice, and ignorance folly, infatuation and darkness.

Bhagavad Gita

Virtue consists in avoiding vice, and is the highest wisdom.

Horace

Get wisdom: and with all thy getting get understanding.

Proverbs

What's been said is enough for anyone with sense.

Plautus

By wisdom a house is built, and by understanding it is established; by knowledge the rooms are filled with all the precious and pleasant riches. A wise man is mightier than a strong man; and a man of knowledge than he who has strength.

Proverbs

Laws are like spiders' webs: if some poor weak creature comes up against them, it is caught; but a bigger one can break through and get away.

Solon

Just as treasures are uncovered from the earth, so virtue appears from good deeds, and wisdom appears from a pure and peaceful mind. To walk safely through the maze of human life, one needs the light of wisdom and the guidance of virtue.

Buddha

Philosophy, rightly defined, is simply the love of wisdom.

Cicero

Heaven's eternal wisdom has decreed that man should ever stand in need of man.

Theocritus

We are more curious about the meaning of dreams than about things we see when awake.

Diogenes

To enjoy good health, to bring true happiness to one's family, to bring peace to all, one must first discipline and control one's own mind. If a man can control his mind he can find the way to Enlightenment and all wisdom and virtue will naturally come to him.

Buddha

Know thyself.

Temple of Apollo at Delphi

Thou, man, alone canst speak.
Wonder at thy glorious prerogative;
and pay to Him who gave it to thee
a rational and welcome praise,
teaching thy children wisdom,
instructing the offspring of thy loins
in piety.

Akhenaton

Philosophy, rightly defined, is simply the love of wisdom.

Cicero

In seeking wisdom thou art wise; in imagining that thou hast attained it—thou art a fool.

The Talmud

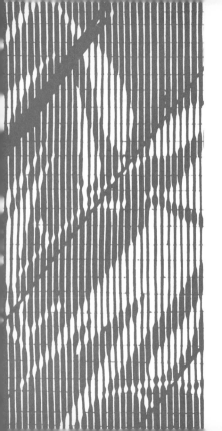

A short
saying oft
contains
much
wisdom.
Sophocles

**I grow old
ever
learning
many
things.**
Solon

By three methods we may learn wisdom: first, by reflection, which is noblest; second, by imitation, which is the easiest; and third, by experience, which is the bitterest.

Confucius

True wisdom consists not in seeing what is immediately before our eyes, but in foreseeing what is to come.

Terence

Wisdom is the conqueror of fortune.

Juvenal

Probable impossibilities are to be
preferred to improbable possibilities.

Aristotle

He whose wisdom exceeds his
works, to what may he be likened?
To a tree whose branches are
numerous but whose roots are few.
The wind comes along and it
uproots it and it sweeps down.

The Talmud

Perfect wisdom has four parts:
Wisdom, the principle of doing things
aright.
Justice, the principle of doing things
equally in public and private.
Fortitude, the principle of not fleeing
danger, but meeting it.
Temperance, the principle of subduing
desires and living moderately.

Plato

Call no man happy till he dies, he is at best but fortunate.

Solon

The fool who knows his foolishness,
is wise at least so far, but a fool
who thinks himself wise, he is called a
fool indeed.

The Dhammapada

Wise men talk because they have something to say; fools talk because they have to say something.

Plato

Wise men learn more from fools than fools from the wise.

Cato the Elder

Let them hate, so long as they fear.

Accius

And those people should not be listened to who keep saying the voice of the people is the voice of God.

Alcuin

Even God cannot change the past.

Agathon

**Whenever God prepares
evil for a man, He first
damages his mind.**

Sophocles

Plato is dear to me, but dearer
still is truth.

Aristotle

To be fond of learning is near to wisdom; to practice with vigor is near to benevolence; and to be conscious of shame is near to fortitude. He who knows these three things knows how to cultivate his own character.

Confucius

Give me chastity and continency—but not yet!

St. Augustine

As one acts and conducts himself so does he become. The doer of good becomes good. The doer of evil becomes evil. One becomes virtuous by virtuous action, bad by bad action.

Upanishads

Never less idle than when wholly idle, nor less alone than when wholly alone.

Cicero

He whose fear of sin takes precedence over his wisdom, his wisdom will endure; but he whose wisdom takes precedence over his fear of sin, his wisdom will not endure. He whose works exceed his wisdom, his wisdom will endure; but he whose wisdom exceeds his works, his wisdom will not endure.

The Talmud

History is philosophy from examples.

Dionysius of Halicarnassus

If I am not for myself who is for me; and being for my own self what am I? If not now when?

Hillel the elder

Everything flows and nothing stays.

Heraclitus

Just as a flower which seems beautiful
and has color but no perfume, so are
the fruitless words of the man who
speaks them but does them not.

The Dhammapada

Heaven and Earth are not ruthful;
To them the Ten Thousand Things are
but as straw dogs.

Lo Tse

Once sent out a word takes
wing irrevocably.

Horace

Lovely it is, when the winds are churning up the waves on the great sea, to gaze out from the land on the great efforts of someone else.

Lucretius

Whom the gods love dies young.

Menander

Anyone can stop a man's life, but
no one his death; a thousand doors
open on to it.

> Seneca

He who cheats with an oath
acknowledges that he is afraid
of his enemy, but that he thinks
little of God.

> Plutarch

Let him who desires peace, prepare
for war.

> Vegetius

A living dog is better than a dead lion.

Ecclesiastes 9:4

The teachings of elegant sayings should be collected when one can. For the supreme gift of words of wisdom, any price will be paid.

Nagarjuna

Proverbial
Wisdom

Drink is the curse of the land. It makes you fight with your neighbor. It makes you shoot at your landlord. And it makes you miss him.

The wind in one's face makes one wise.

**Pride goes before destruction, and
an haughty spirit before a fall.**

The older the fiddle the sweeter the tune.

What's good for the goose is good for the gander.

A stitch in time saves nine.

If you lie down with dogs you'll rise with fleas.

Boast not of tomorrow; for who knows what tomorrow may bring.

Wisdom excels folly, as far as light excels darkness.

There never was an old slipper but there was an old stocking to match it.

Firelight will not let you read fine stories, but it's warm and you won't see the dust on the floor.

It's no use carrying an umbrella if your shoes are leaking.

The best way to keep loyalty in a man's heart is to keep money in his purse.

Humor to a man is like a feather pillow. It is filled with what is easy to get but gives great comfort.

A trout in the pot is better than a salmon in the sea.

One pair of good soles is better than two pairs of good uppers.

New brooms sweep clean.

Least said, soonest mended.

One beetle
recognizes another.

He that repeats gossip separates friends.

Answer not a fool according to his folly.

A silent mouth is sweet to hear.

A nod is as good as a wink to a blind horse.

No matter how often a pitcher goes to the water it gets broken in the end.

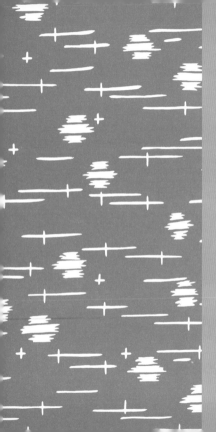

There are
finer fish
in the sea
than have
ever been
caught.

You'll never plough a field by turning it over in your mind.

The old pipe gives the sweetest smoke.

You must crack the nut before you can eat the kernel.

Every patient is a doctor after his cure.

Neither give cherries to pigs nor advice to fools.

All marriages are happy. It's having breakfast together that causes the trouble.

A scholar's ink lasts longer than a martyr's blood.

Take gifts with a sigh, most men give to be paid.

A wounded spirit is the heaviest load to bear.

A good name is rather to be chosen than great riches.

Riches make themselves wings.

As cold waters to a thirsty soul, so is good news from a far country.

Only a fool is scornful of the commonplace.

Ask no questions, hear no lies.

Wisdom and virtue are like the two wheels of a cart.

Wise is the man who has two loaves, and sells one to buy a lily.

Great wits have short memories.

The jealous ear hears all.

Seize the day!

**If there was no low there would be
no high.**

The best wine comes out of
an old vessel.

Trouble brings experience and experience brings wisdom.

Good broth may be made in an old pot.

An old cart well used will outlast a new one abused.

An old ox makes a straight furrow.

Where age is evil youth can learn no good.

One man's meat is another man's poison.

Fortune favors fools.

Better be a fool than a knave.

Young men think old
men to be fools, and
old men know young
men to be so.

The fool asks much, but he is more fool who grants it.

Once mad never wise.

He has great need of a fool, that plays the fool himself.

He is a fool that forgets himself.

Make not a fool of yourself to make others merry.

He is a fool that thinks not that another thinks.

Wise men make proverbs and fools repeat them.

A fool believes everything.

Wise men learn from other men's harms; fools by their own.

A fool and his money are soon parted.

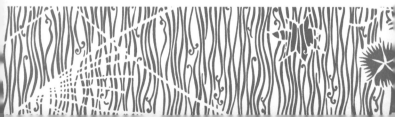

Better not promise,
than to promise and
not pay.

Only fools rejoice at promises.

The sleep of a laboring man is sweet.

In the day of prosperity be joyful, but in the day of adversity consider.

A man hath no better thing under the sun than to eat, and to drink, and to be merry.

Be not curious in unnecessary matters: for more things are shown than men understand.

Don't be made a beggar by banqueting upon borrowing.

The stroke of
the whip
maketh marks
in the flesh; but
the stroke of
the tongue
breaks bones.

Envy and wrath shorten the life.

An empty vessel makes the most noise.

If fools didn't go to market, bad wares would not be sold.

A bird in the hand is worth two in the bush.

Every beetle is a gazelle in the eyes of its mother.

A fool's tongue is long enough to cut his own throat.

Every ass likes to hear himself bray.

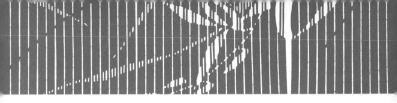

Lend only that which you can
afford to lose.

Don't judge by appearances.

A fool may give a wise
man counsel.

A fool may ask more questions in an hour than a wise man can answer in seven years.

There is no rest for the wicked.

Folly and learning often dwell together.

The devil will find work for idle hands to do.

Children and fools have merry lives.

He that digs a pit shall fall into it.

He that watches the wind shall not sow; and he that watches the clouds shall not reap.

All good things must come to an end.

When the blind lead the blind both will fall into the ditch.

Don't count your chickens before they hatch.

A truly great man never puts away the simplicity of a child.

A trouble shared is a trouble halved.

**Believe nothing of what you hear,
and only half of what you see.**

Eat to live, do not live to eat.

Learning is a
treasure which
accompanies its
owner everywhere.

A still tongue makes a wise head.

Keep something for a rainy day.

More haste less speed.

Love righteousness, ye that be judges of the earth.

A merry heart makes a cheerful countenance.

Moderation in all things.

Old sins cast long shadows.

You can't please all of the people all of the time.

Fools live poor to die rich.

You can lead a horse to water but you can't make him drink.

Learn to walk before you try to run.

Keep your mouth shut and your eyes open.

If you play with fire you will get your fingers burnt.

Honesty is the best policy.

He that is his own lawyer has a fool for a client.

A good scare is worth more than good advice.

It will all be the same in a hundred years.

He travels fastest who travels alone.

Knowledge is the mother of all virtue; all vice proceeds from ignorance.

He that knows little, often repeats it.

Good fences make good neighbors.

Don't judge by appearances.

Throw enough dirt and some of it will stick.

Out of debt, out of danger.

Out of sight, out of mind.

The road to hell is paved with good intentions.

Time and tide wait for no man.

Thoughts to Live by

I have learned throughout my life as a composer chiefly through my mistakes and pursuits of false assumptions, not by my exposure to founts of wisdom and knowledge.

Igor Stravinsky

Each of us is the author of our own story and there's a new page to be written every single day.

To those with wisdom, happiness is not about getting what you want, it's about wanting what you've got.

You cannot shake
hands with a
clenched fist.
Indira Gandhi

**Learn from the
politician. When
you throw dirt at
those you oppose
all you do is lose
ground.**

Choose to
be positive.

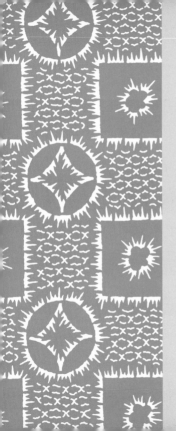

Whatever
you do, the
world is
watching.

If you wish
to be
understood,
say exactly
what you
mean.

We cannot do great things.
We can only do little things
with great love.

Mother Theresa

It is wiser to concentrate on the effort not the outcome.

The wise know that patience will often achieve far more than force.

I don't think it would be wise to place four hundred people in a metal tube with wings and send it into the air.

I don't think it would be wise to place a family in a metal box on wheels and send them down flat surfaces at 70 mph.

I don't think it would be wise to try and get to the moon.

I don't think it would be wise to try and open a man's chest and fiddle with his heart.

It is just as important to follow your dream through the bad times as the good times.

Success never comes to look for you while you wait around.

Anyone is entitled to have their opinion of you, but do not take it to heart. It is your own opinion of yourself that matters.

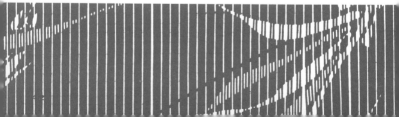

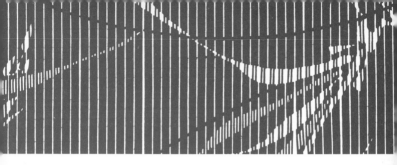

Forgiveness is not an occasional act; it is a permanent attitude.

Don't get bogged down in what the critics have to say.

Every single day great
things are done by
ordinary people.

**What is right is not
always popular but
it would be unwise
to do what is not
right, however
popular it might be.**

Success lies in
everyone.

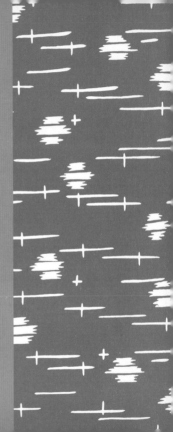

You win some.
You lose some.
You wreck some.

Research it. Plan it. Do it.

It is no one's destiny to fail.

Be young now. You can always start growing old later.

Why rush? Consider the diamond. It began as a patient lump of coal.

It is not the mountain we conquer but ourselves.

Sir Edmund Hillary

What one man greets with friction the other turns into momentum.

Never place business before family and friends.

If you jump to conclusions you are likely to hurt yourself in the fall.

Life is not a matter of chance, it's a matter of choice.

It is far
wiser
to
know
than
to be
known.

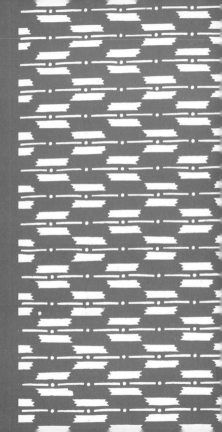

Sometimes, in the company of others, you have to imagine yourself as you are when there's nobody else around.

Ask yourself in everything you do, is it better than just good enough?

Many seek an easier life, but those who succeed seek to become stronger people.

No man can know where he is going unless he knows exactly where he has been and exactly how he arrived at his present place.

Maya Angelou

Try not to miss out on any of the adventures offered by life.

The first thing that the adventurer conquers is himself.

It is perfectly possible to die at a ripe old age and never to have lived at all.

Memories are great, but never let them cast their shadow across your dreams.

The wise laugh often
and much.

The wise gain the respect
of the intelligent.

The wise look for the beauty in everything.

The wise try always to find the best in others.

The wise strive to leave the world a better place.

Difficulty is a fine catalyst
for miracles.

The caterpillar's end is the
butterfly's beginning.

It is vital to remember
that the easiest person to
deceive is oneself.

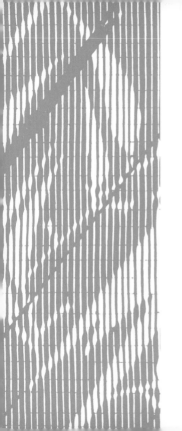

The meaning of life is that nobody knows the meaning of life.
Woody Allen

If even just one other life has in any way benefited from your actions, then you can know your life has been successful.

Never use yourself as your own role model.

Some people try to learn in days what it takes others years to understand. Days teach little, years teach much.

Everyone in a team is of equal value.

Look back on
your life.
Now look ahead in
your life.
Now look inside
your life.

A boring day is a day lost forever.

It is the runner who leads the race that sets the pace for the rest of the pack.

The worried man who can manage a smile will unnerve his enemies more than the cowering wreck.

To punish me for my contempt for authority, fate made me an authority myself.

Albert Einstein

The wise find at least one reason to laugh each day—even if it's at themselves.

In much of life we strive to hide our mistakes, whereas the artist in his wisdom is selective and exhibits his.

Everyone has past misfortunes, just as everyone has blessings.

Science may have found a cure for most evils, but it has found no remedy for the worst of them all—the apathy of human beings.

Helen Keller

We do not plant trees for ourselves, but for posterity.

Be prepared to take a risk—wait for the perfect moment and it will never arrive.

Appreciate the kindness of others, but never rely on it.

Perfection has one
grave defect; it is apt
to be dull.

Somerset Maugham

**Lessons learned
are the bridges with
which to cross the
rivers of regret.**

Try to avoid speaking in anger, a hasty word can never be retrieved.

If you have one aim in life, let it be to fullfill your potential.

The wise know the value
of kindness.

**Gratitude transforms
what we have into enough,
and more.**

Gratitude can turn a meal
into a feast.

Don't judge each day by the harvest you reap, but by the seeds you sow.

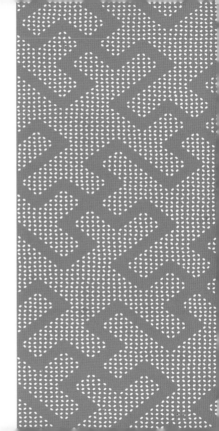

It is unwise to harbor the thought that you are not as good as others. Others will take your word for it.

Only with wisdom can you see that belief in what you do not see can lead you to see what you believe. Some call this faith.

It is when you feel most like giving up that you are closest to your goal.

So cheat your landlord if you can and must, but do not try to shortchange the Muse. It cannot be done. You can't fake quality any more than you can fake a good meal.

William S. Burroughs

Those who do not want to imitate
anything, produce nothing.

Salvador Dali

Neither success or failure is
ever permanent.

Trouble is an inevitable part of life, as is your power to defeat it.

The wise way to solve a problem is not through worry.

If you allow others to anger you, then they have conquered you.

Do not fear fear, it is
a survival instinct—
use it as such.

Fear is a central part of wisdom,
to feel no fear leads many into
foolish actions.

Waste no tears over the griefs
of yesterday.

Euripides

It is a glorious feeling to be able to
rise again after a fall.

If I have the belief that I can do it, I shall surely acquire the capacity to do it even if I may not have it at the beginning.

Mahatma Gandhi

It doesn't have to be dark for you to reach for the stars—they are always out there waiting to be touched.

Don't get bogged down in concerns for what you have tried and failed. It is far better to concern yourself with what it is still possible for you to do.

The best gift we will ever receive in this life is ourself.

Don't ask of others what you are
not willing to do yourself.

The worst failure is the
failure to try.

Sometimes you have to make the choice between not finishing many things and finishing a few.

No one can become great without first becoming good.

Don't think that if only a few complain
then most are happy.

**The wise man sees as much as he
ought, the fool tries to see as much
as he can.**

Kill off the past and we kill off the future.

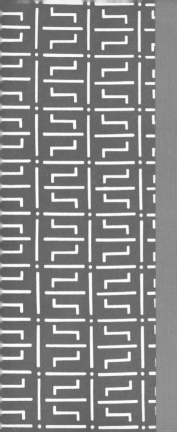

A well-placed pat on the back when things go right will achieve more than bellowing at fifty people when something goes wrong.

Wealth is no measure of success in life.

Success isn't about where you are in life. It is about the obstacles you've overcome.

In life there should be no half measures—go all the way.

You must learn to accept yourself before you can expect others to accept you.

Only dead fish swim with the stream.

Why should it be that the three most difficult admissions are "I'm sorry," "I was wrong," and "I love you"?

You can never expect to be able to control what goes on outside if you are not capable of controlling what goes on inside.

Don't expect more than you would be willing to give.

No totally honest person can say that they were always happy. Life is made up of happy and sad moments, one cannot exist without the other, just as there cannot be light without dark.

It is not being able to give the right answer that shows wisdom, but being able to ask the right question.

All artists dream of a silence which they must enter, as some creatures return to the sea to spawn.

Iris Murdoch

The intention makes the lie, not the words.

Words are the most
powerful drug used
by mankind.
Rudyard Kipling

Why do we tend to disbelieve all facts and theories for which we have no use?

Wisdom can only be acquired by an inquiring mind, if you don't ask the questions you won't receive the answers.

Our life is what our thoughts make it. Learn to discipline your mind.

A man who does not think for himself does not think at all. Thinking cannot be done by proxy.

No one can expect to understand all that life has to show them.

Only with confidence comes strength.

Never be afraid of your own ideas.

There is little to be valued as highly as your good name, it is something that once lost is impossible to replace.

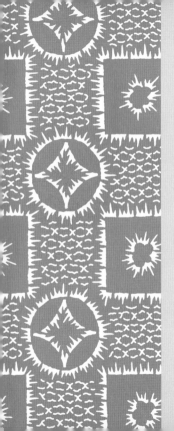

Chances are that
what you put off
today, you will also
put off tomorrow.

**If you can
recognize the need
for improvement
things are already
improving.**

You can do anything,
the only limits are set by
your own imagination.

The future you
get was paid for
somewhere in
your past.

Published by MQ Publications Limited
254–258 Goswell Road, London EC1V 7RL
Tel: 020 7490 7732 / Fax: 020 7253 7358
e-mail: mqp@btinternet.com

Copyright © MQ Publications Limited 2000

Text © David Baird 2000
Design concept: Broadbase
Design: Susannah Good

ISBN: 1-84072-119-7

1 3 5 7 9 0 8 6 4 2

All rights reserved. No part of this publication may be reproduced or transmitted
in any form or by any means, electronic or mechanical, including photocopy,
recording, or any information storage and retrieval system now known or to be
invented without permission in writing from the publishers.

Printed and bound in China